By Shante Stoner

Copyright Page © 2021 by Shante D. Stoner

All rights reserved. No part of this publication may be reproduced, distributed, or transmitted in any form or by any means, including photocopying, recording, or other electronic or mechanical methods, without the prior written permission of the publisher, except in the case of brief quotations embodied in critical reviews and certain other noncommercial uses permitted by copyright law. For permission requests, write to the publisher, addressed "Attention: Permissions Coordinator," at the address below.

Printed in the United States of America

First Printing, 2021

Last Update, 2022

Mailing Address:

BlackLight Logistics LLC

304 S Jones Blvd Suite #3314

Las Vegas, NV 89107

www.blacklightlogisticsllc.com

Disclaimer: *If you follow anything I've mentioned here, or use any forms I've sent, it's at your own discretion and I won't be liable for any outcomes. I am not a lawyer or an accountant. This info is for informative purposes only and is based on **my** knowledge and experience.*

Contents

Who can we dispatch for? 6

Signing Up a Driver 9

Know how you'll get paid 16

Day to Day Operations 19

Truck Types 40

Palletized vs. Floor 43

Weight Restrictions 45

How you get paid 49

As far as what we paid to setup our business… 52

Marketing 56

Final Thoughts 59

So first, let's touch on the benefits of why a truck driver needs a good dispatcher:

While a driver can go on load boards themselves and book loads, using a dispatcher is more efficient for business. While they have to stop and look for loads from wherever they are, plus call up brokers on each load they like, plus negotiate with them (do some calculations to get the best rate), plus receive and fill out all the paperwork to move the load for the broker, it's a lot while they're trying to move quickly or get into a rhythm and maximize their time.

As we know, if they're not driving, they're not making money. Having a dispatcher decreases their down time because we can be looking for loads while they're still driving, plus pre-plan for the next load once we know where they'll be when it's time to get rolling again. We can have loads lined up for them.

Who can we dispatch for?

Me and my husband have started a small trucking company in a box truck while we work our way up to a semi (most likely a Power Only unit) so my angle is from being a dispatcher for our company. However, you can use dispatching as a business and find drivers who need help.

They have to have their own authority; they cannot be leased on to someone else's authority. If there is one independent truck driver – since they're a one-man show, we can help them tremendously. Or a small fleet of trucks – as some small fleets don't have their own dispatch department.

Be mindful that large fleets do tend to have their own dispatch department, so they probably won't use you. I wouldn't spend too much energy on going after them.

Since different people may have different reasons for reading this book, I'll talk to you about things you'll want to consider as far as starting your own dispatch business as well as you just dispatching for your own truck(s).

But since this is meant to emphasize your day-to-day operations actually dispatching there will be more emphasis on that throughout the book.

Signing Up a Driver

Again, I've only dispatched for our truck (as of the time of writing this) but if you're starting your own dispatch business, you'll need a process for signing up drivers.

You'll have to have them sign a Carrier Packet. This will help you understand their needs as a driver. You want to know what type of equipment they have, their truck type, trailer, additional permits, do they have straps, load bars, where they want to run, etc.

Because when you go to book a load, if it requires specific equipment, the broker will ask you if the driver has it. You will know, based on how they fill out this packet.

For example, if it's a flat bed, the broker may ask 'Does your driver have tarps and how old are they, or what condition are they in?' and so on...

You will also need their basic business information: Motor Carrier Authority Number (MC#), business contact information, you can ask them if they need help invoicing or if they use a factoring company that is already doing that.

You'll want them to sign the power of attorney, it's a limited one, so it just gives you the right to find loads under their MC# and negotiate on their behalf with the brokers for the load rate and fill out the broker packets on their behalf.

You can also ask for their factoring information in the packet. If the driver uses a factoring company, you'll want to access that account to run credit checks on brokers and make sure their particular factoring company will give the green light to pay on the load. And if the driver wants, you can also submit the proper paperwork to request payment once a load is delivered.

That's usually the **SIGNED** Bill of Lading (BOL) and a copy of the Rate Confirmation. It could also include lumper receipts or anything else related to the load. I'll explain those later.

Outside of those specific forms, you're wanting to know the general information. Where is the truck? Where do they want to run? Stay within their state, or go wherever they can get the most pay? What is the minimum rate they will accept (it's usually a price per mile)? Are there any states they don't want to run in? and so on...

When they send your packet back, you'll want them to send you a copy of their MC Authority, current Certificate of Insurance and a copy of their W-9.

Whenever you, as the dispatcher, fill out a contract with the broker, they'll need these documents. So keep them in a folder, ready to download and send for each load that's booked with a new broker.

Remember that if you've booked a load for a truck with a broker before, they'll already have the driver's information. But every time you book a truck with a new broker, you have to fill out a new packet and you'll need all of this information.

Consider online software that will allow you to make this process as easy as possible, like using some 100% electronic forms so the driver doesn't have to print your packet out and fill it out by hand and then scan it and email it back to you. If they can just type all of their information in and then sign and send it back electronically it'll be easier on them. This lower barrier to get started will give you an advantage over drivers who don't make this process quick and easy.

Look into SignRequest, DocuSign or JotForm to get your search going.

*One VERY Important Thing I want to point out...

As a dispatcher, you cannot find loads, book them, hold them and then start soliciting those loads to your driver pool. Never book a load unless you have a driver that you were searching for a load for, and you're booking it for them specifically. Don't waste peoples' time.

NEVER book one load for one driver under another driver's authority number! If you have more than one driver, they all need to have their own **active** authority and you need to have a system where you keep all of their information and documents separate.

So when your day starts, go down your list and search for loads for one truck at a time.

Pull up one truck with their MC# and find them a load under **that** MC# and then move on to the next driver with their own MC# to find a load and book it under their MC#.

Don't get yourself or your driver or the broker into trouble by doing your job irresponsibly. If someone doesn't have their authority, the FMCSA thought they shouldn't so don't try to help them out by booking loads under another driver's authority and jeopardizing their good standing. That can devastate a business and it's just simply not fair or good business on your part.

Here are some screenshot pages from a carrier packet that I put together:

CONTRACT PAPERWORK

Email:  *com – Fax*:

Dear Carrier,

I have attached a Dispatcher's Carrier Contract for Service. Please read, sign and return.
I also need the additional items below to setup your file.

1.) Operating Authority (Motor Carrier Certificate/USDOT Certificate)
2.) State DOT Certificate of Registration (if applicable)
3.) UCR
4.) Insurance Certificate of Liability Insurance
5.) W-9
6.) Completed Contract/Agreement
7.) Completed Credit Card/Debit Card Authorization Form
8.) Limited Power of Attorney

All information should be faxed or emailed to above correspondence information.

Thank you,

TRUCK AND AVAILABILITY INFORMATION

Company Name
_____

Contact Person
_____

Email_____
_____

Phone _____

Fax# _____

Emergency Contact
_____ Phone _____

Physical Address
_____

City _____ State _____ Zip
_____

Mailing Address
_____

City _____ State _____ Zip
_____

MC# _____ USDOT# _____

EIN/SS# _____

Business Type: _____

IND SOLE PROP ___ PARTNERSHIP ____ S/C CORP ____ LLC ____ OTHER ________

Check all states you have your authority in:

AL ____ FL ____ KY ____ MO ____ NJ ____ PA ____ VA ____

AR ____ GA ____ LA ____ MS ____ NM ____ RI ____ VT ____

AZ ____ IA ____ MA ____ MT ____ NV ____ SC ____ WA ____

CA ____ ID ____ MD ____ NC ____ NY ____ SD ____ WI ____

CO ____ IL ____ ME ____ ND ____ OH ____ TN ____ WV ____

CT ____ IN ____ MI ____ NE ____ OK ____ TX ____ WY ____

DE ____ KS ____ MN ____ NH ____ OR ____ UT ____

In Which States Do You Prefer to Operate:

_____
_____
_____
_____
_____

Areas You Do Not Travel:

_____
_____
_____
_____
_____

YOUR EQUIPMENT PROFILE

TRUCK#
_____
TRIALER#_____

**TYPE OF TRAILER   MAX LOAD WT   LENGTH
OF TRALER   # OF TRAILERS**

FLATBED_____   _____   _____
_____   _____

DRY
VAN_____   _____   _____
_____   _____

BOX
TRUCK_____   _____   _____
_____   _____

HOTSHOT_____   _____   _____
_____   _____

18

RATE INFORMATION

What is your desired Rate Per Mile $_____
Deadhead Included: YES____ NO____

What is your **Minimum** Rate Per Mile for Front Haul $
_____

What is your **Minimum** Rate Per Mile for Back Haul $
_____

Max# of Picks _____ Max# of Drops _____

Cost Per Extra Stop_____

Please check available attributes: Tarps ____ Straps ____ Chains ____

Binders ____ Pipe Stakes ____ Dunnage ____ Pallets ____ Ramps ____

Pallet Jack ____ Load Bars ____ Lift Gate ____ Dock Height ____

Airride____ Vented____ Pads____ Ramp____

Do you have a TWIC card? Y ____ N ____

Do you have a SCAC Code? Y ____ N ____ If yes, list SCAC code# _____

Do you have a Hazmat/Smartway Certification? Y ____ N ____

Do you haul Permit/Oversized loads? Y ____ N ____

Driver Touch (Y/N) _____

Max Weight You're Willing to Haul _____

Do you desire Full-time ____ or Part-time ____ Dispatching Services?

If you have multiple drivers:

Run Loads by YOU____   OR   Run Loads by the Driver____

Preferences:

Longer Hauls _____   OR   Shorter Hauls _____

Higher Rate Per Mile_____   OR   More Miles Per Day/Week_____

FACTORING INFORMATION

If you use a factoring service, please provide us the following information. This will ensure that we only use brokers that are approved by your factoring company.

Factoring Company_____

_____
Contact
_____
_____

Phone_____
Fax_____

Email_____

Website_____

Billing Address_____

City_____ State_____ Zip Code_____

Login Site (if applicable)
_____

Login Name: _____ Login Password_____

INSURANCE INFORMATION

Please note: We do require our carriers to maintain a minimum of $1 Million in Liability and $100,000 in Cargo Insurance.

Insurance Company_____

Contact_____

Phone_____ Fax_____

Email_____

Address_____

City_____ State_____
Zip Code_____

MULTIPLE TRUCK OPERATION FORM

Please complete this section if you are a trucking company with more than one (1) truck working under your authority, that you require dispatching services for.

Truck 2

Driver First and Last Name: _____ Driver Phone: _____

Trailer Length: _____ Trailer Width: _____ Trailer Height: _____

Max weight of load: _____ Truck #: _____

Type and number of tarps: _____

Amount of chains: _____

Ramps: YES___ NO___   TWIC: YES___ NO___

Mileage Distance willing to travel: _____

Areas you do not travel:
_____
_____
_____

Truck 3

Driver First and Last Name: _____ Driver Phone: _____

Trailer Length: _____ Trailer Width: _____ Trailer Height: _____

Max weight of load: _____ Truck #: _____

Type and number of tarps: _____

Amount of chains: _____

Ramps: YES___ NO___   TWIC: YES___ NO___

Mileage Distance willing to travel: _____

Areas you do not travel:

_____
_____
_____

Truck 4

Driver First and Last Name: _____ Driver Phone: _____

Trailer Length: _____ Trailer Width: _____ Trailer Height: _____

Max weight of load: _____ Truck #: _____

Type and number of tarps: _____

Amount of chains: _____

Ramps: YES___ NO___   TWIC: YES___ NO___

Mileage Distance willing to travel: _____

Areas you do not travel:

_____
_____
_____

Notes:

1. Does the assigned driver have the right to make load decisions for you?

   _____

2. Does the driver need to have a copy of the load confirmation?

   _____

3. Do we need to do the initial dispatch of the driver, or will you?

   _____

4. Other:

   _____
   _____

Rules for Service

- DISPATCHER WILL MAKE 100% EFFORT TO KEEP TRUCK/TRUCKS LOADED
- TRUCK WILL BE CALLED & OFFERED LOAD WHEN EMPTY
- IT WILL BE STRICTLY UP TO THE DRIVER TO ACCEPT OR DECLINE THE LOAD
- THE DRIVER IS RESPONSIBLE FOR ANY LOADING AND UNLOADING FEES FOR THE LOAD HE/SHE IS HAULING
- THE DRIVER IS RESPONSIBLE FOR ACQUIRING ANY NECESSARY LICENSES OR PERMITS FOR LOADS
- THE DRIVER IS RESPONSIBLE FOR CONFIRMING THAT THE FREIGHT LOADED ON HIS/HER TRUCK IS THE CORRECT FREIGHT
- THE DRIVER IS RESPONSIBLE FOR CONTACTING THE DISPATCHER ONCE LOADED
- THE DRIVER IS RESPONSIBLE FOR CONTACTING THE DISPATCHER WITH ANY PROBLEMS PERTAINING TO THE LOAD
- THE DRIVER IS RESPONSIBLE FOR ADHERING TO ALL CRITERIA OF THE LOAD WHILE IN HIS/HER POSSESSION
- THE DRIVER IS RESPONSIBLE FOR PICKING UP AND DELIVERING THE LOAD ON TIME
- THE DRIVER IS RESPONSIBLE FOR CONTACTING THE DISPATCHER ONCE HE/SHE HAS UNLOADED
- !!!ADDITIONAL BILLING SERVICE INCLUDED!!! UPON RECEIPT OF POD AND RATE CON FOR EACH LOAD, DISPATCHER WILL CREATE INVOICE AND SEND BROKER/SHIPPER/FACTORING COMPANY A COPY OF SAID INVOICE, POD AND RATE CON VIA EMAIL OR FAX.
- IF ADDITIONAL ROADSIDE SUPPORT SERVICE IS ACCEPTED, DISPATCHER WILL HAVE 24/7 AVAILABILILTY TO SUPPORT DRIVER IN FINDING ASSISTANCE IN ROADSIDE EMERGENCY SITUATIONS.

I
_____
_ have read and understand the rule and agree to the terms of these rules for services.

CREDIT CARD AUTHORIZATION FORM

PLEASE PRINT OUT AND COMPLETE THIS
AUTHORIZATION AND RETURN TO US.

All information will remain confidential.

Cardholder Name:
_____

Billing Address:
_____
_____
_____

Credit Card Type: _____ Visa _____ MasterCard _____ Discover

Credit Card Number:
_____

Expiration Date:
_____

Card Identification Number (last 3 digits located on the back of the credit card):
_____

Amount to Charge: as per valid agreement between Cardholder and ███████████ C. I authorize ███████████ C to charge the agreed amount listed above to my credit card provided herein. I agree that I will pay for this purchase in accordance with the issuing bank cardholder agreement.

Cardholder – Print Name, Sign and Date Below:

Signed: _____

Print Name:
_____

Dated:
_____

LIMITED POWER OF ATTORNEY

BE IT KNOWN, that

_____(your name) with MC# _____and DOT# _____ has made and appointed, and by these presents does make and appoint _███████████████████ and lawful attorney for _____(your company), place and stead, for the following specific and limited purposes only:

To contract loads and to perform all acts and things necessary to contract loads.

giving and granting said attorney, full power and authority to do and perform all and every act and thing whatsoever necessary to be done in and about the specific and limited premises (set out herein) as fully, to all intents and purposes, as might or could be done if personally present, with full power of substitution and revocation, hereby ratifying and confirming all that said attorney shall lawfully do or cause to be done by virtue hereof. This power of attorney is to remain in full force until revoked by me in writing and received in mail or email by _____ to the company mailing address or the company email address.

Company Name: _____
Company Owner Signature: _____
Printed Name: _____
Title: _____ Date: _____

Witness Signature: _____
Printed Name: _____
Date: _____

Again, these are screenshots so it wouldn't work as a straight download but it will give you an idea of how you could build out your Carrier Packet for signing on new drivers.

The more information you can get, the easier it will be for you to do your job.

Once you have all of the CMV (Commercial Motor Vehicle) information, the driver's running preferences, their minimum rate per mile, factoring information, special permits, and business information, you'll be able to complete any carrier packet.

Some are more like online registration systems where you fill in the information and some are actual PDF's that you'll have to download or print, fill out and send back.

This should be a good starting point for you gather the driver's information.

Now I'm going to show you some example screenshots of an actual Broker Carrier Packet. After you've negotiated a good load, the broker will send you a packet where you will provide them with all of the driver's trucking company information. I want you to see how all of the information you collect from the driver will come into play when you're filling out the paperwork for each broker they run for. You'll fill it out and send it back to get the Rate Confirmation (I'll show you one of those in a few pages as well.

This is not the full packet. There were some pages with the "agreement terms" that I left out so that there wouldn't be too many inserts here. However, I've included all of the pages that you'd have to fill out or sign. The only thing additional would probably be adding initials on the other "agreement terms" pages.

Montreal, QC
Vaudreuil, QC
Richmond Hill, ON
Toronto, ON
Vancouver, BC

Calgary, AB
Chicago, IL
Springfield, MO
Atlanta, GA
Salt Lake City, UT

CARRIER PROFILE

Company Name: _____ Telephone: _____
Physical Address: _____ After Hours: _____
_____ Fax : _____
_____ E-Mail: _____

Remit Address: _____ MC # : _____
_____ CDN Authority: _____
_____ FEIN #: _____
EDI   Yes _____ No _____ SCAC Code: _____

Qualifications

CTPAT :   YES: ____ NO: ____   SmartWay :   YES: ____ NO: ____
ELD Compliant: YES: ____ NO: ____   Carb Tru: YES: ____ NO: ____
ELD Producer: _____   HazMat: YES: ____ NO: ____

Trailer Types

of Tractors: _____   # Flatbed: _____
Dry Van: _____   # Step-Decks: _____
Reefer: _____   # Tankers: _____

Broker Reference

Company Name: _____   Company Name: _____
Contact: _____   Contact: _____
Telephone: _____   Telephone: _____

Company Name: _____   Company Name: _____
Contact: _____   Contact: _____
Telephone: _____   Telephone: _____

PAYMENT OPTIONS APPLICATION

CARRIER INFORMATION

COMPANY NAME	
ADDRESS	
TELEPHONE #	FAX #
MC #	

AUTHORIZATION

OFFICER NAME	
EMAIL	TITLE

PLEASE SELECT AN OPTION:

A	QUICK PAY 5% PAYMENT IN 48-72 HOURS
B	QUICK PAY 2.5% PAYMENT IN 7 DAYS
C	EFT OPTION (CDN$ or US$)
D	ACH OPTION (USA DOMICILED)
E	FACTORING COMPANY (Please provide NOTICE of ASSIGNMENT)
F	COMCHECKS (5%) *
G	CHECKS

A copy of a voided company check is required for Option A, B, C, D

* If you select this option, you will need to contact your dispatcher for payment.

TERMS AND CONDITIONS

1. For all the payment options, ▇▇▇▇▇ion Service▇▇▇▇▇▇") must have on file a copy of our carrier contract signed by an officer of your company;
2. Carrier must provide ▇▇▇▇▇uments pertaining to the load (invoice, bills of lading, delivery receipts, etc.), showing delivery without loss, damage or delay. POD's must be legible and without overages, shortages or damages and must have the receiver's signature or stamp. Failure to submit appropriate documentation may result in a delay of payment. Documentation received outside of business hours will be considered received the following business day;
3. For Options A & B, all payments made will reflect the carrier's invoice is discounted by 5% or 2.5% accordingly for utilizing ▇▇▇▇ Quick Pay service;
4. For Options A & B, in order for processing of the invoice, ▇▇▇ must receive the above mentioned documents by fax @ ▇▇▇-▇▇▇-▇▇▇▇ or email ▇▇▇▇▇▇▇▇nsport.com.
5. For Options C to G, in order for processing of the invoices ▇▇▇ must receive the above mentioned documents by fax @ 8▇▇-▇▇▇-▇▇▇▇ email P▇▇▇▇▇▇▇t.com. It's also possible that another email address or fax will be given to you by your dispatcher for specific requirements.
6. ▇▇▇ill hold all of the above information provided in the strictest confidence. Such information will only be utilized by ▇▇ to make eligible payments to the applicant as agreed.

Signature needed   Print name:
_____   _____

AGREEMENT FOR MOTOR CONTRACT CARRIER SERVICES

THIS AGREEMENT ("Contract") is made and entered into this ___ day of ____ 20__, by and between ▇▇▇ Transportation Services (USA), Inc., a Delaware corporation ("Broker"), and _____ a company with its principal place of business at _____ (Street address), _____ (City), ____ (State) _____ (Zip) ("Carrier"). The foregoing named parties are sometimes subsequently referred to herein collectively as "the Parties" and individually as "the Party."

RECITALS

WHEREAS, Carrier is a motor contract carrier of property, duly registered with the Federal Motor Carrier Safety Administration ("FMCSA") in Docket No. MC-_____, and is engaged in the business of transporting property by motor vehicle in interstate, intrastate, and foreign commerce;

WHEREAS, Broker is duly registered as a property broker with the FMCSA in Docket No. MC # ▇▇▇ and arranges transportation of property by motor carriers for its customers; and

NOW, THEREFORE, in consideration of the foregoing premises and the mutual promises contained herein, the Parties agree as follows:

TERMS AND CONDITIONS

1. **Contract Term and Termination.** This Contract shall be effective as of the date written above and shall remain in effect until terminated in the manner provided herein. Either Party shall have the right to terminate this Contract at any time upon thirty (30) days' prior written notice to the other Party.

2. **Shipments to be Tendered by Broker.** Broker hereby agrees to tender shipments to Carrier as Broker's needs require for transportation in interstate, intrastate or foreign commerce, and Carrier hereby agrees to transport such shipments in accordance with the terms and conditions stated in this Contract. The Parties acknowledge and agree that this is not an exclusive arrangement, meaning that Broker shall not be required to submit any or all of its transportation requirements to Carrier, and Carrier may provide transportation services to other customers, provided that Carrier complies with Paragraph 22 of this Contract. Each shipment tendered by Broker and accepted for transportation by Carrier shall be confirmed via a "Master Load Tender Confirmation" ("Load Confirmation"). Each Load Confirmation shall be governed by the terms and conditions of this Contract.

3. **Determination of Carrier's Compensation.** Carrier shall seek payment for services rendered hereunder solely and exclusively from Broker, and shall not, under any circumstances, present an invoice, bill, demand, or other claim for payment to Broker's customers or any consignor or consignee of a shipment tendered hereunder. Broker shall compensate Carrier as set forth below:

    a. Broker shall pay Carrier in accordance with rates and charges set forth in the Load Confirmation, which rates and charges are mutually agreed upon and apply to all shipments tendered under this Contract.

    b. With respect to its rates and charges, Carrier agrees that the Load Confirmation shall control and that none of its tariffs, circulars, pricing authorities, and/or similar documents shall apply to the transportation

Carrier Initial _____
Date _____

against Carrier arising from Carrier's breach of this contract, Broker shall be entitled to recover its reasonable attorneys' fees if Broker prevails in such litigation.

14. Bills of Lading/Receipts. Carrier shall issue and sign a standard bill of lading or similar receipt ("Receipt") acceptable to Broker and Broker's customer upon acceptance of a shipment for transportation. The terms and conditions of such Receipt shall not modify, supplement, or supersede the terms and conditions of this Contract, unless specifically agreed to by Broker in a separate signed writing, apart from the Receipt. Carrier's issuance and execution of the Receipt shall constitute prima facie evidence that Carrier received the shipment in good order and condition, unless exceptions are specifically noted. Carrier shall submit an original copy of the Receipt to Broker evidencing delivery of the shipment, unless otherwise instructed by Broker, in which case Carrier shall retain custody of the Receipt and provide it to Broker upon request. Carrier assumes all risks and liability arising from its loss of any Receipt issued hereunder. This Paragraph shall survive termination of this Contract.

15. Subcontractors. Carrier shall not co-broker or subcontract any shipment tendered hereunder without first obtaining prior written authorization from Broker. Carrier shall remain fully liable to Broker under the terms of this Contract for any work or service performed by any of its agents or subcontractors in connection with a shipment tendered hereunder, whether the agent or subcontractor is known or unknown to Broker. Carrier shall indemnify, defend, and hold Broker and its customer harmless from and against any Damages of any kind made by or against any such agent or subcontractor. On any occasion when Carrier seeks to co-broker or subcontract a shipment by seeking prior written authorization from Broker, it shall provide proof of the subcontracting carrier's operating authority, its "satisfactory" safety rating, and its insurance in the forms and amounts required of Carrier in Paragraph 13 hereof. This Paragraph shall survive termination of this Contract.

16. Communications. Carrier and Broker shall seek to communicate by the most efficient means to exchange information useful or necessary to achieve for performance of this Contract. Such means shall include without limit telephone, fax machine, e-mail, Internet, electronic funds transfer, EDI, and satellite.

17. Assignment. This Contract may be assigned only upon the express written consent of both Parties, which consent may be withheld for any reason. If assigned pursuant to the terms of this Paragraph, then this Contract shall inure to the benefit and be binding upon the assignee. Any assignment that is not in full conformity with this Paragraph shall be null and void.

18. Notices. Except for routine communications made in the course of performance of this Contract, all notices shall be in writing and delivered by facsimile, certified mail, or express mail. Notices transmitted by facsimile shall be deemed received as of the date and time of sender's fax transmission report indicating successful transmission. Notices transmitted by certified mail or express mail shall be deemed received as of the date and time signed for by recipient. Notices shall be addressed as follows:

To Broker: ███████████████
█████████vd., Suite 250
██████, QC H4N 3M9
Attention: Carrier Relations

To Carrier: Carrier Name _____
Address _____
City, State, Zip _____
Attention: _____

Carrier Initial _____
Date _____

26.   Entire Agreement and Merger. This Contract, the Appendices attached hereto, and any Load Confirmations constitute the entire agreement between the Parties, and supersede all previous communications, statements, representations, writings, and instruments with respect to the subject matter hereof. This Contract may be modified, supplemented, or amended only through a writing executed and agreed to by the Parties.

27.   Secured Load Policy. As set forth on Appendix B to this Contract, which Appendix is attached hereto and incorporated herein, this Contract has a secured load policy in place for all loads that are to be secured with seals or padlocks and Carrier must adhere to these strict secured load policies set forth by Broker during the term of the Contract. Secured loads are to be treated with the highest priority in maintaining the integrity of the load as well as protecting the product from adulteration. The Secured Load Policy in Appendix B provides further explanation.

28.   Choice of Law. This Contract shall be governed by and construed in accordance with the laws of the State of Kansas without regard to rules relating to conflict of laws. Any lawsuit concerning the interpretation, performance, enforcement of this Contract shall be brought in either the state or federal courts located in Jackson County, Missouri, or Wyandotte County, Kansas, and the Parties irrevocably consent to the jurisdiction of such courts. This Paragraph shall survive termination of this Contract.

IN WITNESS WHEREOF, the Parties have caused this Contract to be executed as of the date and year first written above.

Carrier
By: _____   By: _____
     (Must be signed by an officer)   (Company officer)

By: _____   By: _____
          (Please print)   (Please print)

TITLE: _____   TITLE: _____

DATE: _____   DATE: _____

Carrier Initial _____
Date _____

APPENDIX B

SECURED LOAD POLICY

Companies are taking extra precautions regarding contamination of their products - beginning with raw materials that are transported.

If upon delivery by Carrier, the trailer seal is broken without the receiver's authorization, they may consider the product possibly damaged and/or tampered with. Their Quality Control (QC) and/or Quality Assurance (QA) people may be called and the shipment(s) may be refused for non-compliance of "TRUCK DRIVER SEAL RESPONSIBILITY" as outlined below.

CARRIER REPRESENTS AND WARRANTS THAT IT WILL TELL ITS DRIVERS NOT TO BREAK ANY SEAL AT ANY TIME AND THAT THE RECEIVER IS THE ONLY PERSON ALLOWED TO BREAK SEALS. IF THERE IS SOMEONE REQUESTING A DRIVER TO BREAK A SEAL OR ANYONE ELSE BREAKS THE SEAL - THE TRUCK DRIVER AND CARRIER ARE TO CONTACT FLS IMMEDIATELY.

Carrier represents and warrants that it will comply with the following "TRUCK DRIVER SEAL RESPONSIBILITY" policy. Please sign and fax back to 8▓▓▓▓▓▓▓▓

- DRIVERS MUST VERIFY SEAL # UPON LOADING AND VERIFY # MATCHES SEAL # ON BOL.
- DRIVERS MUST CALL IN SEAL # PRIOR TO LEAVING SHIPPER A ▓▓▓▓▓▓▓▓ (24hrs)
- DRIVERS MUST CHECK CALL DAILY AND VERIFY SEAL IS STILL IN TACT
- DRIVERS MUST CALL IN UPON DELIVERY; VERIFING SEAL WAS BROKEN ONLY BY RECEIVER AND SEAL # MATCHED # ON BOL

In the event of a broken security seal, the load may be turned away and rejected by the consignee. This includes unreadable numbers or non-matching numbers with the BOL. The receiving manager will be notified along with the carrier's dispatcher and a representative from the facility where the load originated.

Pertaining to an inspection where the seal must be broken, the truck driver is responsible to have the authorities indicate, **by stating directly on the BOL**, that the seal was broken in their presence.

THE FOLLOWING INFORMATION MUST BE CALLED IN IMMEDIATELY ▓▓▓▓ at ▓▓▓▓▓▓▓▓
- LOCATION OF SEAL BEING BROKEN
- AGENT/OFFICER NAME
- AGENT/OFFICER BADGE NUMBER
- PHONE NUMBER OF AGENCY AND/OR LOCAL AUTHORITY

Truck driver is responsible to have the authorities re-seal the truck with their authorized own seal and identify doing so directly on the BOL.

If seal must be broken for any reason – truck driver and carrier are responsible to contact 24-hour on-call person at ▓▓▓ immediately at ▓▓▓▓▓▓▓▓

This process will help secure all products during transportation and will remove all unnecessary risks to the customers, suppliers, carriers, and ▓▓▓ We appreciate your cooperation.

Signed By: _____ Broker Name ▓▓▓▓▓▓▓▓ on Services (USA), Inc.
Name: _____ Title: Director Carrier Relations_____

Carrier Name: _____
Signature: _____ Date _____

Print Name: _____ Title: _____

Carrier Initial _____
Date _____

Ok, I'm about to insert some screen shots of a real Rate Con. So at this point, you've gathered the information from your trucker. Then you've searched for a load and checked with "this trucker's" factoring company to make sure they will pay on "this trucker's" load with "this" particular broker. Then you've filled out their Broker Carrier Packet. Now, they will send you the Rate Con. This confirms the load is indeed your trucker's load and they can head to the pickup.

Make sure you have this before they head to the pickup. Some brokers are shady unfortunately and will cancel your load and give it to another driver that they got to take it for less.

Once you have the Rate Con though, the load is yours. You'll usually have to sign the Rate Con and send it back to the broker too.

Rate Confirmation for PO# 17097741

Please look for more available loads at www.

PLEASE USE THIS AS YOUR INVOICE AND SEND THIS WITH YOUR PAPERWORK

Contact		
Jo		
Phone:	8206	
Email:		
Fax:		
Office Staffed 24/7		
P.O.	5150	

This confirmation is an agreement between ____ner to haul the indicated load at the indicated rate, and is not a dispatch. If load is changed or canceled ____ ruck order not used" will be paid unless the carrier has been dispatched. Car____ for dispatch, which includes pick up number, shipper name/address, and directi__
** Carrier or its agent certifies that any TRU equipment furnished will be in compliance with the in-use requirements of California's TRU regulations.

Carrier Contact Info				Carrier Responsible For	
Blacklight Logistics Llc (ia)		Phone:		Unloading:	None w/ valid unloading receipt
	BOX 206773	Fax:		Pallet Exchange:	None
	773	Dispatcher:		Estimated Weight:	44000
Terms: 28DAYS		Driver:			
		Truck #:	/Trailer#:		

Name	Rate	Type	Unit	Quantity	Total
Blacklight Logistics Llc (ia)	$600.00	Line Haul	Flat	1	$600.00
				Total:	**$600.00 USD**

Rates that are based on weight or count will be calculated from the quantities loaded.

Load Information:

Trailer Type:	Van			
Trailer Size:	53 ft	Temperature:	(Continuous)	
Hazmat:	Non-Hazardous	Pallet/Case Count:	0 pallets/0 cases	

Note To Carrier:

All drivers are required to sign the BOL upon delivery. The date, printed name, & signature of the person receiving the load must be on the BOL or $75 penalty. $150 TONU if load cancels after 30 minutes from being dispatched. In & out times are required on the BOL for any detention requests to proceed. Excessive late fee's may apply if load is delivered late. $500 fine if a solo driver is put on a team requested load. Pictures of the signed BOL are due upon delivery.

Pick-up Location	Date	Time
Cedar Rapids, IA	05/17/2021	asap

Delivery Location	Date	Time
Waverly, IA	05/17/2021	FCFS 0800-1500
Cedar Rapids, IA	05/17/2021	RIGHT AFTER

All Accessorial charges must be pre-approved. Unauthorized charges may not be paid, not all detention requests will be honored. BROKER must be notified 30 minutes before CARRIER is requesting detention reimbursement. Carrier must also get the agreed detention amount in writing. Detention is on a per load basis and variable rates may apply.

Invoice Information:	This document is also your invoice to ▮▮▮
	If this box is checked, carrier is required to mail original paperwork to ▮▮▮ e below address. Otherwise, carrier can email (▮▮▮om) or fax ▮▮▮ 2) paperwork or use TRANSFLO Express® truck stop scanning.
CARRIER INVOICE #	If you would like a **Quick Pay** on your load and we do not require original paperwork, please write "1 Day Quick Pay" or "7 Day Quick Pay" on your invoice and send to Quickpa▮▮▮ ▮ or fax to ▮▮▮

	Mail Address:	**For Overnight Delivery:**
TRANSFLO Express:	▮▮▮	▮▮▮
$3.00 per load charge	PO Box 9▮▮▮	
Use this document as your cover page	▮▮▮ 0209-0049	

Welcome to TRANSFLO Express®

▮▮▮ contracted with TRANSFLO Express® to get your documents in easier and with more certainty than in the past. With this new service, you will be able to get your trip information to us in a matter of minutes instead of days. Just follow the instructions below to get paid as quickly as possible! As soon as you are finished with you▮▮▮ d, head to a participating truck stop with your paperwork.

Use the first page of this ▮▮▮ ate confirmation as your cover page! (the bar code ensures the paperwork comes ▮▮▮

Tape any receipts or other small documents onto a blank piece(s) of paper. Be sure to remove any staples or paper clips and take care to not mark on or near the bar codes. Take your papers and use the self-serve TRANSFLO kiosk, or hand them to the cashier who will scan all of the documents. You will receive a receipt that contains a unique confirmation code that allows you to view your documents online at www.transfloexpress.com up to 14 days from the day they were sent.

A fee of $3.00 per load will be taken out of your final pay so you don't have to worry about paying at the truck stop. If you send multiple scans for the same load, you will be charged for each scan.

▮▮▮ o accepts paperwork sent from your office computer using TRANSFLO $Velocity software, use our broker ID of ▮▮▮

THIS AGREEMENT IS SUBJECT TO THE TERMS OF THE BROKER/CARRIER AGREEMENT SIGNED BY THE CARRIER ▮▮▮ THIS AGREEMENT CONSTITUTES AN ADDENDUM TO THE BROKER/CARRIER AGREEMENT. THIS RATE QUOTE IS INCLUSIVE OF ALL CHARGES UNL▮▮▮ KE ORAL AND WRITTEN OBJECTIONS TO ITS TERMS WITHIN TWENTY-FOUR (24) HOURS AFTER RECEIPT (EMAIL j▮▮▮.com OR FAX ▮▮▮ . IF WE DO NOT RECEIVE SAID OBJECTIONS YOU HAVE AGREED TO THESE TERMS.

▮▮▮ PO# 17097741

_____
CARRIER REPRESENTATIVE SIGNATURE

Know how you'll get paid

Will you send an invoice via PayPal or another invoicing system and wait for payment or will you use something that's called a Virtual Terminal? With invoicing, you simply send your driver an invoice at the end of the week (or whatever day you choose) with the loads you've booked for them and then they will pay it.

With a virtual terminal, you can send the driver a credit card authorization form along with your carrier packet that they will fill out. They'll provide you with their card details and sign a document authorizing you to charge it on the days you provide them.

You'll enter their information into your virtual terminal and then you can run the card on the designated payment dates. You'll just have to send them an invoice or document as well, letting them know of all of the charges for that week.

Square has one that's free upfront, the fees are deducted from payments, but their fee is higher than some other virtual terminals. It's convenient to start with because they're reputable and the system is very easy to use but do some research and find the best option for you. Be mindful of contracts with early termination fees and such.

Day to Day Operations

Once your driver has signed up with you and you have all of their information and running preferences, you can begin to search for their preferred loads.

Keep in mind that new drivers could possibly have a hard time finding good loads. When they have new authority, they have no credit for a broker to verify that they're credible and will deliver their loads safely and on time. For that reason a huge bulk of brokers will not work with a driver whose authority is under 30, 60 or 90 days old. (It's not impossible by any means but be prepared).

In the Facebook groups we're in, people have graciously provided lists of brokers and shippers they know of who will work with new authorities so I would network and grab those to keep as a reference. I always screenshot them in my phone when I see them.

I would do some due diligence when you have down time and call some of those brokers to confirm instead of waiting until you have a driver to find out.

Now you have some options in terms of searching for loads. Most people start with the load boards. The longer you're in the business and can make contacts, you may develop relationships with brokers to where you can have a relationship with them to get info on good loads for your drivers.

If you're not already making those contacts, use the load board at first, but do that in the process of booking loads. Ask questions like, do you normally have freight on this lane? If so, my driver runs this route so let me know when you have another one and we can see if he's available.

As long as the driver is getting loads delivered on time and running safely, brokers would probably like to have them move more loads for them.

If you have broker contacts, call the ones in the area where your truck is and see if they have anything, if not…load boards, lol.

As far as load boards go, this depends on which board you're on. I'm going to talk about DAT because that's the one I'm familiar with. I plan to use DAT Power because they actually have live load updates and more tools to help the drivers (in my opinion), but Truckers Edge is great too! I would advise you to either go to their website or YouTube and become very familiar with the load board and how to navigate it. It's fairly simple but very informative.

There's a link to my "over the shoulder dispatching mini eCourse" at the end of this book. I'll give you a tutorial of the DAT Power software and you can see the process of how I search for loads, what tools I'm using and a document of what to say to brokers when you're on the phone. Check it out after you're finished with this book to see a good daily workflow.

Look at a few things. First, they have a tool that tells you how many loads are currently available going into each state and leaving out of each state. Use that to determine if you have room for negotiations.

If your driver is going into a state that has a lot of loads but fewer trucks, you have room to negotiate because the trucks are in demand. If it's the opposite, not so much, because they can find anyone you know.

Also, this will tell you if it's okay to take a load because you'll want to make sure you can get them a load leaving the area as well. Sometimes there's a great load going into an area, but you end up having to take a lower rate to get out. Do your research ahead of time so that you can use that to negotiate a higher rate going in. This is also a lookout for the driver, which is your main priority. They may not mind running a load into an area of the pay is higher because it'll cover the deadhead miles coming out.

Another feature, you can go to the search and type in your truck type and equipment, what city and state the truck is in and where the driver wants to go (if they don't care, leave this field blank so you can see everything).

When that info populates, you'll see available loads with broker information, and you can start making calls. Before you do, check the other feature on the side that tells you about the average rate for loads similar to the one you're looking at from the last 2 weeks or 30 days (depending on which subscription you have). You can use that to determine if the load is listed for a fair rate or if you have room to negotiate. This is a golden tool for beginners.

Now we can delve into the actual planning part. If you can only find partial loads or something like that, see if the driver has time for multiple stops along the way. They also have a feature (I think it's in DAT Power though) where you can see other loads along the route and possibly call to book those too. If you do try to put more than one load on a truck, be sure it's ok with the broker. Sometimes the shipper will only allow for their freight to be on a truck. If that's the case, you can't do multiple loads on one delivery.

Aside from all that, you can see where your truck is and where they're going. Go to Google and calculate the distance. Divide the cost of the load by the distance and see what the rate per mile is. Refer back to your Carrier Profile Packet and make sure the load is at least paying what the driver wants.

Before you start calculating, consider the difference between deadhead miles, total miles and loaded miles, as your driver may have requirements for each one separately or just miles as a whole.

Loaded miles refers to the number of miles the truck is going once it's actually loaded with the freight, from the shipper to the receiver's drop off location.

Deadhead miles refers to the distance the truck will drive from where they are currently sitting empty, from there to the shipper's location to go and pick up the load.

Total miles refer to the total amount of the miles they'll be driving altogether from where they are sitting to picking up the load and then delivering it.

Snapshot of what this looks like:

A load picks up 30 miles away from where the truck is currently parked. So the truck leaves where they are and then drives for 30 miles to the pick-up location. At the pick-up location the truck gets loaded. Once they leave the pick-up location and are fully loaded, they drive 70 miles to the drop-off location and get unloaded.

In this example:

Deadhead miles = 30 (they drove for 30 miles with nothing on the truck)

Loaded miles = 70 (they drove for 70 miles while the truck was loaded)

Total miles = 100 (they drove a total of 100 miles on this particular load)

For the sake of round numbers, let's say the driver was paid $200 for this load

$200/100 (miles) = $2 / mile

The driver was paid $2 per mile as far as total miles goes.

If they had only driven the 70 miles they would have made closer to $2.85 per mile. Keep in mind that most loads are posted and calculated by the brokers based on loaded miles. They have no idea where a truck is that will be picking up the load, so it makes sense you know.

This is the reason why drivers like to deadhead as few miles as possible, it maximizes their profit margin so always search for the load closest, that stands to make the most amount of money.

Let's look at a different, general example with some round numbers.

Example:

Load is going 400 miles and it's paying $1,200.

$1,200 / 400 = $3 per mile. So if the driver's minimum was like $2 per mile or $3 per mile, you know this is an acceptable load. If it was like $5 per mile, you know it's not and they won't run it. $5 may be kind of high and dramatic for my example, but you get what I'm saying.

I don't think anyone's minimum is $5 but this is just a simple example. Nevertheless, try to stay within the driver's rate per mile because they know how much they need to operate their truck.

If they're new and they don't know, educate them on finding out so they know which loads they should take and which ones they should pass on.

If you have to negotiate try to start high so that maybe you can meet in the middle and get your driver the minimum. Don't start *unreasonably* high or the broker may not even consider your offer because they'll know you don't know what you're talking about.

More considerations, the hours of service. From what I learned in my course (yes, I took a dispatching course when we started our business and it was great, I'll link it at the end) don't expect the driver to drive more than 700 miles in a day, 500 to be on the safe side.

Also, just become familiar with how drivers run and what they're comfortable with.

So while you're calculating the load miles and pick-ups and drop offs, be sure you plan for them to be able to safely and legally deliver on time.

Hours of service, as of today, state that a driver has a total 14-hour work clock from the time he starts his ELD (Electronic Log Device - logs his daily mileage) and is rolling. Within those 14 hours, he can only be driving for 11 hours. Getting loaded doesn't count toward the driving hours so they can use some of that in the 3 hours outside of drive time. However, it does count toward the total 14 hours.

If you're confused by the Hours of Service (HOS) read the details on the FMCSA website before you start looking for drivers because you have to know this.

So even if a driver spends 5 hours getting loaded, he still only has a total of 9 hours to get to his destination or somewhere to pull over for the reset which is 10 hours before he can start driving again.

So total "On-Duty" time is 14 hours, only 11 of that can be drive time and then they must stop and take a 10-hour break before they can start driving again.

Speaking of pick up and drop off. You have 2 types. A fixed time or an open window. If you see a load and it has a specific pick-up time, you need to make sure that from whatever distance the truck is currently sitting, they have enough time to get there by that time.

It may say by "X" time like 5:00 or if it's an open window it might say anywhere from 5pm – 8pm. Be mindful of that when you're booking loads and when you're pre-planning. Even though we want to look for the next load, we must look at all hours-of-service rules, how fast the truck can drive (because some semis may be governed at like 60 mph), and make sure they can meet the drop off time.

Sometimes if they get there late, they can get pushed to the back of the line for getting loaded or unloaded which could throw off their time if you've pre-planned another load. Keep all of these considerations in mind.

Okay so now that we have some info on what to look for to load the driver, let's get into the next part. Once you find the load, now you have to run the brokers credit and make sure they get the green light from the factoring company to be able to have them pay on the load.

If your driver uses Triumph, who DAT partners with, you'll see a green check next to loads that they will factor so that's pretty easy. If they use a different factoring company, go into that account and run the broker's credit. All factoring companies pretty much offer this feature so their drivers will know who's credible *with them* and who they'll advance the load on. So just because one factoring company says yes, it doesn't mean another will. So you have to check with each factoring company that each of your drivers is using. If you get the green light, then call.

ALWAYS check first! If that driver uses a factoring company, they need them to pay on the invoice to get paid quickly. If the factoring company doesn't approve of a broker, they will not pay the driver for that load.

After you negotiate the load, book it. If your driver requires you to check with them first, verify that they want to take the load. If they say you can book it as long as it meets their minimum and where they want to go, then just book it. Those loads can go away quick!

The broker will run the MC# of your driver, so have it handy. If they agree to have them move it, they'll send you an email with their broker carrier packet. You fill it out and send it back to the broker. Broker will send you the Rate Confirmation. This has the pick-up and drop off times and locations. They'll usually want you to sign it. Do that and send it back to them.

Then relay this info to your driver as soon as possible so they can start planning their trip. Send them a copy of the Rate Con.

You keep in contact with the driver throughout the delivery to be sure they don't have any issues with delivering the load. The broker may check in with you to see where the truck is at and make sure things are on schedule, check in with the driver so you can let them know. Always keep the broker updated to maintain a good rapport.

If you have software that tracks the driver's location, that you have access to, you can use that. I know they all have to have ELD's and most of them have GPS, but I don't' know yet if there's a way for you to have access to that information, unless they give it to you or provide you with their login info on the software.

I know there is some dispatcher software on the market that probably has an app for your drivers to download to make this easy. I just haven't tried them yet so I can't say personally.

If you're dealing with a big brokerage, a lot of them have apps where they want the driver to check in with the times they arrive at their stops and leave so that they can track when loads are being picked up and dropped off. And some even require the driver to be tracked by them. If so, they'll ask you for the driver's cell phone number so they can send them their tracking app. If they require it, the driver ***will be required*** to download that app and allow themselves to be tracked until they drop that load off.

Be available for issues. If there's unexpected traffic going through a downtown area this could throw off the arrival time, if there is an accident on the highway with stop and go traffic, this could throw off the arrival time, if there is severe weather and the driver needs to pull over to wait it out, this will throw off the arrival time, if they get a tire blow-out or another unexpected mechanical issue to where they have to pull over and wait for break down, this will throw off your arrival time. You get my drift, lol.

Advise your driver to let you know if anything like this happens, or if they simply get tired and have to pull over for a while. Then you will have to update the broker on their status and new ETA.

Most brokers will be okay as long as they know what's going on so just keep them in the loop.

Remember that most of these guys are independent just like you and they need to be able to keep their shippers updated on where their freight is. So work together on that.

Once the load is delivered, the driver will get the Bill of Lading signed (this must happen, or load will not get paid!!) They'll send you a picture of the BOL and the Rate Confirmation. If this is something you're offering to do for the driver, you will submit it in their factoring account and the factor will pay on the load. If not, just send the broker the signed BOL so they'll know the load was delivered and is complete.

Lots of factoring companies have mobile apps, so the driver may submit the pictures directly to them through the app on their phone. Discuss that with the driver but still get a copy for your records and keep it so you know that the load was delivered.

Now you're ready to stay on deck for the next load. Also, when you're pre-planning, you can post trucks. So like, if you know the driver will be available the day after tomorrow, post their truck on DAT or whichever load board you choose with the details of the truck and where it'll be to see if any brokers need it and reach out to you.

Here are some **talking points with brokers when you're booking the load**. Ask:

Is the load still available?

Can you verify the pick/up and delivery times and locations?

Is there an appointment time or an open window, on the pick/up *and* the delivery?

What is the weight, length, commodity on the load?

Is it palletized or floor loaded?

How much are they willing to pay on the load?

Employ sales tactics

Ex: Rate says it's $950. Say "I need $1200 to move it."

Then if they say, "I can do $1050" Say "Can you hold on while I verify that with my driver?"

Then come back and say "Okay, the driver will take it" and move forward with booking the load.

Start high. **If the rate is acceptable**, you can ask for more.

If it's good, take it.

If it's too low, thank the broker and move on or say "any chance I can get it for…. (whatever your minimum is)." If it's still low, move on.

See if the client accepts the rate (it could be below their minimum for different factors, such as seasonal reasons or a shift in the economy) – at this point, tell your client this. If your client is not okay with that, like seasonal rates, ask them if they prefer a different lane for now or if they want to wait the season out?

Over time, you'll get a feel for the lanes and seasons, so you'll become familiar with these things.

Truck Types

Different types of trucks carry different types of freight. Consider this when you're looking for loads as there are some load boards that specialize in certain types of freight. I'll give you a few common ones to start off, but there are more.

Dry Van - Most common type, carries dry goods on a 53 ft. enclosed trailer

Power Only - Refers to a semi that just has a tractor (the front part, lol). They go pick up loaded trailers, containers, empty trailers, etc. and drop them off and then keep moving. With big brokerages, they be required to get one of their empty trailers to bring into the shipper to leave before they can pick up the loaded one. Keep that in mind as far as trip planning and time because you never know where they'll have to go to pick up the empty trailer first.

There are also "load out" trailers listed on load boards. This is where the driver can pick up that empty trailer, use it for a set number of days to run "dry van" freight and then drop it off wherever the load stated.

Keep in mind you can run Power Only loads with a Day Cab or a Sleeper. The Day Cab weighs less, is shorter and may be used more for shorter hauls that can be completed in one shift, so the driver doesn't end up with a possibility of needing to sleep with no bed. The sleeper is the semi with a bed in the back.

Flat Bed - They have an open flat trailer usually used for bulky and oversized loads that can't fit into an enclosed trailer

Reefer - (Refrigerated Unit) - this one is temperature-controlled, enclosed, usually for transporting groceries and medicine and other items that need to be kept cool. You may be able to find some dry goods loads to fit depending on the dimensions so it can be a versatile option

Box Truck - Enclosed trailer, carries dry goods, good for partial loads, boxes can vary from 9 ft to 14 ft, to 20 ft, 24 ft and 26 ft. Those are the most common lengths.

Palletized vs. Floor

Palletized means the load is on pallets and may be easier and quicker to load because they can use forklifts. That also means to make sure that the width of the load can fit on your truck, as far as being loaded by a forklift. This more so applies if you have a box truck.

We've had to turn down loads due to this issue. Our width was good, but with the forklift having to load the pallets, it was too close as far as the measurement goes, so we couldn't pick the load up.

If its **Floor-Loaded,** this means it will be loaded by hand, piece by piece, box by box and will take longer (so take that into consideration when booking a load and looking at the times).

Weight Restrictions

I know box trucks, and they have a max capacity at 26K lbs. generally (not all, the CDL ones go up to 30K I believe). Weight is extremely important!!! I have to stress that. If a driver gets pulled over and they're overweight, they can get huge tickets from the state troopers and possibly get stopped in their tracks (put out of service) because they can't run heavy. They lose time and money.

You'll have to know the weight of your truck (or your driver's truck) empty and then calculate what the load is listed for by subtracting it from the weight of the truck to make sure the load is not too heavy for the driver. I just googled it, a 26ft box truck weighs 12,990 empty (give or take I'm sure because ours is 16K so get this from the driver).

Ex: load says it's 10,000 lbs. truck is governed at 26,000 pounds but it weighs 12,000 pounds empty. You can pay to use the scale at any truck stop to check the weight of an empty or loaded truck.

First 26,000 (full capacity) – 12,000 (empty weight) = 14,000 (so this is how much the load can weigh for a driver to accept it).

Now, even though we know the truck can carry a load of 14,000 to be legal, drivers do not like to haul at the max amount because it's too easy to be overweight after they get loaded. They'd rather stay on the safe side.

So let's say you see two loads and one is 14,000 but one is 12,000 pounds, they'd prefer to take the load for 12,000 (within reason of the load amounts) and be safe with their carrying capacity weight. But you can ask them for their preference with max weight, this way you'll know it when you're looking for a load.

These examples were for a box truck, the max weight for a 53ft trailer with the semi is 80,000 pounds. So you'll have to start there and see what it weighs empty to see how much weight you can accept on a load. Google is telling me; it weighs somewhere between 14-16,000 pounds but that could be for a day cab. I think semis with a sleeper are closer to 30,000 – 40,000 so just check with your driver on their empty truck weight specifically.

How you get paid

We talked about how you can bill, but let's touch on this again real quick. Some factoring companies (maybe very few because I think it's new) will have an option to pay the dispatcher. Basically once they get the information to pay on the load, they'll send the dispatcher their fee and then send the driver the rest.

More commonly, you will have to bill for it. What I learned as the better option of the two, is to bill each week for the previous week's loads. Any loads booked Sunday – Saturday will be billed on the following Monday. You determine what your preference is for that.

If you'll use like Square or PayPal or something, create your invoice and email it to the driver so they can pay on it when it's time. Be sure to list the loads they're paying you for.

If you go the virtual terminal route, again, consider looking into options. You do have to have a business bank account and your EIN so I would set your business up before setting this up. You cannot open a business banking account without an EIN. It's free to get on the IRS website though.

As far as what we paid to setup our business...

$99 - I got an LLC. I used Zen Business (I can't remember if it was $100 or $150 but I did get a Partnership LLC for me and my husband and I got it expedited so the fee may be different for you). Or you can do it on your own, if you know how, on your Secretary of State website.

Like I said, me and my husband started a trucking business, so this is why we opted for the LLC. You may want to start as a sole proprietor for free and then get an LLC later if you choose or you can get your LLC straight out of the gate. Even if you set up an LLC it may be good to sit with a tax professional to make sure you're establishing your business in the best way, with the best tax advantages for your particular operation. I found out when filed our taxes for the first time that we didn't really need to go the "partnership" route. But it can be a headache to swap status's so try to make sure you setup the right way from the beginning.

*Side note: if you are a dispatcher only, DAT will allow you to sign up to search for loads for drivers without having to enter an MC# as long as you have a business set up and they can verify it, like with a website or something. Meaning you can sign into your own account to search for all of your drivers and even before you get one, to get familiar with it. So consider that as well when you're deciding on getting the LLC or not. Otherwise, you will need your drivers MC# to search for loads for them on most load boards.

$0 - I applied for my own EIN on the IRS website for free

$48/year - I created my website on Wordpress.com

$0 - I created an email with Gmail. It's like $6/month for the Business Workspace option. Consider doing that to look more professional to get the professional email address instead of the @gmail.com

You can choose to get general business insurance, some places have it for as little as $30 per month.

$10/month - I got a separate business phone number through an app on my iPhone, it's called Sideline

$5/month - I got an app on my iPhone for faxing called FaxDeck

$10 – I got business cards through VistaPrint, I caught it on a sale for 500 for $10 + shipping. If you're familiar with Canva, you can also consider creating a virtual business card instead of having hard copy cards (or in additional to your cards)

Those are the only expenses that I can think of, associated with the dispatching side of our business.

Marketing

As far as finding drivers, I'd set up a website, so you have a web presence and contact form available for anyone interested. Then you can market through social media, whichever platforms you choose, locally and in-person.

I'm currently on Instagram @blacklightlogistics (and yes I've had drivers reach out for dispatching on this platform based on my posts).

You can look on Craigslist and other online marketplaces, truck stops, and anywhere else drivers may be. I also told my husband we'll sign up with the local Chamber of Commerce because they have networking events, and we may come across other small businesses who need help with our 26ft box.

For dispatching, it could also be beneficial. I'd also look into other FB pages for networking (like you're probably already doing, lol) and anywhere else you can think of.

There are a lot of little intricacies in between but this is a start for you. I just wanted you to have a snapshot of daily operations and considerations for dispatching your trucks.

Remember that you're not the only person out here dispatching so try to find creative ways to make yourself stand out and provide good customer service. Be honest, upfront and on time.

Also, consider starting out with one type of truck while you learn the business and then add more on later. Like, become super-efficient in reefers or dry vans or flat beds or box trucks and then stay in that lane if you like it or add on others when you feel comfortable.

Final Thoughts

Lol! I just cheated and added this section...

As I was proof-reading this, a whole wave of things came to mind that I hadn't included but I definitely want you to be aware of. Like I said, this book is mostly based off of my experience with our business and we've had some loads since I've started writing so I want to share a little bit more, bear with me.

As the dispatcher, you will be responsible for asking the broker for any extra fees for situations that come up. One of those may be, **TONU**. This means Truck Ordered Not Used.

If you book a load and show up, but for some reason the load is not ready, was cancelled or rescheduled and your truck will not be picking anything up, you can request payment for TONU from the broker.

It simply means, you did what you were supposed to do, you showed up when you were supposed to and somebody else dropped the ball on your time. TONU prices can vary based on the contract with the broker. Always see if it's in there when you fill out the packets with them. It's usually a flat fee.

Another one is **Detention** pay. If you had an appointment time to pick up the load and it just wasn't ready, you can ask for this pay via the broker from the shipper or receiver. It usually starts after driver has been sitting and waiting for 2 hours or 3 hours and can vary from $25 to $50 per hour in my experience. But the driver had to have been on time to the appointment. This is why those check in times are important to keep track of.

Layover is the next one. This is when the driver is delayed by the shipper or receiver for one or more days. Some drivers are not allowed layover pay until they've been sitting for 24 hours without the load (it depends on what's in the contract). I've seen this be anywhere from $200 to $300 per day.

You as the dispatcher will be the one requesting these fees from the broker. The broker would get the money from the shipper/receiver, so you'll be requesting it from them. For this reason, keep good records about the in and out times.

Make sure your driver texts/emails you as soon as they arrive onsite to pick up or deliver a load and be sure to relay that to the broker *at those times* as well. This way, there is a paper trail for how long a driver has been waiting. Another way to track this easily, is if the driver has like a tracking app on their phone. Some brokers require it to be downloaded while under a load anyway.

Lumper Fees are another one. This fee comes into play when the driver helps load or unload the truck. If you know they'll need to assist in advance, you can ask for this ahead of time. If you don't know until they get to the location, update the broker that the driver had to assist so they can add it into the final payment and adjust the Rate Confirmation if necessary.

This can also pertain to using outside assistance, like paying someone else to load or unload. From what I can see, it's most common with food and grocery distributors than with dry freight.

But we've had to ask for this fee before because my husband helped to unload a couple times so I know it can be used in dealing with box trucks as well.

If this happens to your driver, be sure to have someone on-site write somewhere on the BOL that the driver assisted with loading or unloading so that you have proof that they helped.

Some brokers are not honest and some people at these facilities are not honest, and you won't get the pay if it wasn't known beforehand unless someone there signs their name saying your driver helped.

With any of these "added" circumstances: TONU, detention, layover, lumpers, etc. you'll be requesting a revised Rate Con from the broker with the additional fees. Make sure that's the one that's submitted to the factoring company and sent along with the load paperwork. Otherwise the factoring company could pay you upfront but then the broker "short pays" it on the back end. Then the driver will have that pulled from the money until it gets resolved. So keep your paperwork in order. Here's a screenshot of rates from a Rate Con:

Rates

The rate shown above is the agreed individually determined rate between the parties.
* Except as otherwise expressly stated in the OCA, in the event the terms and conditions of this Tender conflict with the OCA, the terms, conditions and provisions of the OCA shall prevail and take precedence.
* N████████ ██endments to this Tender shall be binding upon ██████████
  si████████████████████████████████████ position o█████
* T█████████████████████████████████████
the OCA.

Accessorials

Accessorials listed apply to domestic over the road 3rd party carriers and are not valid for drayage.

1. Detention with Power
    a. Loads with set appointments: time accrual will begin at the time of scheduled appointment
    b. Time accrues in 15 minute increments
    c. 5 hour maximum of detention per load
        i. First 2 hours Free
            1. No detention provided
        ii. Eligible Detention Hours
            1. $50 per hour if automated
            2. $40 per hour if manually recorded
        iii. If Duration exceeds 5 hours, the charge becomes Layover
2. Layover
    a. Automated $250 per day
        i. $150 per day if manually recorded
    b. Will not be paid detention at same stop
3. Truck Ordered Not Used
    a. Load must be either:
        i. Dispatched & driver enroute/arrived
        ii. Tendered >30 minutes lead time day of pickup
    b. Location Services: $200
    c. No Location Services: $150
4. Stop-off
    a. Post Tender: $50 + Out of Route Miles (OOR)
        i. OOR Dollar per Mile (DPM) would match DPM on load
5. Reconsignment
    a. $75 + OOR
        i. OOR DPM would match DPM on load
6. Driver Assist
    a. $50 per stop
        i. Tailgating only

IF YOU HAVE ANY QUESTI██████████████████████ALS, PLEASE REACH OUT████████████
CONTACT LISTED ON PAGE█████████████████

Also...

Pay attention to instructions from the broker about picking up a load. We had one that picked up at a warehouse in the airport that required you to have a copy of the Rate Con in hand.

I had assumed we could use the electronic one you're emailed (in most cases you can) but we couldn't. So we had to go get a hard copy. I was freaking out because I was like how are we supposed to do that out on the road and with a short time window?

My husband, who is a veteran truck driver told me to calm down, lol, because you can get it from the truck stop. First, locate the nearest truck stop to you. Then you just look on their website or call (I know you can for Pilot locations but unsure of others) and get their email or fax number.

Fax or email the Rate Con and then you can go walk into the truck stop and pay to pick it up. I don't know the cost because my husband went in to retrieve ours but I'm sure it was "change-per-sheet." Then you can take that printout with you to the pick-up.

This is one of the times when our mobile fax service really came in handy. I was able to save the Rate Con to my iPhone in the documents and then upload it into the fax app and send it to the store... But then their fax was down, lol! So I ended up just emailing it from our business email. Like I said, you can always call to see which one is available to you.

So if you need that and you're coming off of a break at a truck stop, just go in and grab it before you head to the pick-up.

If you're dealing with Power Only, be mindful of whether or not you're provided specific trailer numbers or gate codes for pick-ups.

Another random thing...

Keep some blank BOL's on your computer and email a copy to new drivers that sign up with you. Encourage them to always keep extras in case they should need one. We never have, but it was a suggestion from our factoring company so I'm just passing it along. As I mentioned earlier, if you don't have one, and have it signed, that load won't get paid. This is completely up to you, it's not necessary but just an extra look-out for new drivers.

While we're talking about BOL's I think it's important to have a complete snapshot of the process from start to finish. So I'm about to walk you through 3 different things that we've brushed on so that you can see the cycle full circle.

The Life Cycle of a Load in a Snapshot:

- Truck is available for a load
- Dispatcher searches for a load
- Dispatcher finds a load that meets the driver's criteria
- Dispatcher verifies the driver's factoring company will pay this broker by doing a credit check in the factoring company's app/website, or having the driver check
- Dispatcher calls driver to confirm they want the load

- Dispatcher calls broker to negotiate a load price and accepts a good load
- Broker sends Dispatcher a Carrier Packet (for new drivers with them)
- Dispatcher fills out the Carrier Packet according to truck details
- Dispatcher emails the completed packet along with the current MC Certificate, Certificate of Insurance and W-9 for the truck driver to the Broker
- Broker sends Dispatcher the Rate Confirmation for the load - it includes the price load is paying, invoicing details, pick-up and drop-off times and locations, carrier information, broker information. You may need to sign and send back to Broker.
- Dispatcher sends the driver a copy of the Rate Confirmation
- If Factoring Company is involved, Dispatcher or Driver will upload the Rate Confirmation into the Factoring Company's system if it is required for fuel funding...If it is not, this step is not necessary to complete at this time
- Diver heads to the pick-up location
- Driver arrives at the pick-up location and lets the Dispatcher know when they arrive
- Dispatcher lets the Broker know that the Driver has reached the pick-up location
- Driver goes in with their Rate Con and gets a paper copy of the BOL and then gets their truck loaded
- Driver let's Dispatcher know they are loaded and heading to drop-off location
- Dispatcher let's Broker know that driver is loaded and heading to drop-off location
- Dispatcher makes themselves available to driver in the case of delays or emergencies and checks in if Broker requests a location update
- Driver arrives at Drop-Off Location
- Driver let's Dispatcher know that they have arrived at drop-off location and what time they got there
- Dispatcher let's Broker know that driver has arrived at drop-off location
- Driver goes in with their BOL and alerts the facility to begin unloading his truck

- When driver is unloaded, someone at the facility will sign the BOL to complete the load

- Driver let's Dispatcher know they are unloaded and sends a copy of the signed BOL (usually via a picture they took with their phone)
- Dispatcher lets the Broker know that the load is complete and sends them a copy of the signed BOL
- At this time, either Dispatcher or Driver will upload the BOL and the Rate Confirmation (if it wasn't uploaded already) to the site for the Factoring Company so that they can pay on the load
- Driver is done and can move on to their next load or set their next available ETA (Estimated Time Available/Arrival)
- At this point, either the Driver, Dispatcher or Factoring company will send an invoice to the broker for payment of the load so that the Factoring company will get paid. Most factoring companies will do this, but if they do not, the driver can assign the Dispatcher to do this, or they will do it on their own. Then move on to the next load.

So now you've seen the full life cycle of a load, let's see how factoring plays into everything.

A trucking company will use a factoring company if they don't have a lot of money laying around to wait to get paid. You see, once a load is delivered, a broker can take anywhere from 30 to 45 to even 60 days to pay on the load. Since driver's need money right away to continue running their business and paying themselves, they use factoring companies.

A factoring company basically buys the invoice. They pay you the money for the load upfront, but they deduct a small fee (factoring fee is usually a percentage like 2% or 3%) for doing so and then they collect the money from the broker for the load you delivered.

Most factoring companies offer other perks such as fuel discounts. And the way it works is, you swipe a fuel card that they provide when you're at the pump and the savings will automatically be deducted from the transaction, or they'll send it to you in a lump sum per month. Because the card is linked to your bank account with them, they will usually just take the amount you spent for fuel, on designated days throughout the week.

At least, that's how ours works. Check with your driver if you want to know the specifics of theirs, but this part doesn't apply to what you do. The invoicing part is more important for you.

So let's look at the life cycle of that, it's much shorter than the actual load cycle.

Life-Cycle of the Factoring Process:

- Driver has factoring company
- Dispatcher or Driver uses factoring company's credit check system to verify that they are willing to purchase the invoice from this particular broker before a load is accepted
- Load gets accepted
- Driver or Dispatcher uploads the Rate Con

- Driver delivers the load
- Driver gets signed BOL upon load completion
- Driver or Dispatcher uploads signed BOL and any additional documents/receipts necessary for payment (if there were any, like lumper fees)
- Factoring company pays Driver for the load (minus their fees)
- Factoring company then creates an invoice for the load (most will) and sends it to the broker to pay for the total amount of the load
- Broker will pay the invoice to the factoring company within 30, 45 or 60 days (whatever their timeframe is)
- Load Payment Cycle is complete

The driver may have an issue if the broker doesn't pay, and they may even have to pay the money back for the load. It depends on whether they chose a "Recourse" or "Non-Recourse" option. These are details that don't concern you, as it's more so dependent on the stipulations between the factoring company and the driver. I just wanted you to be aware of the cycle.

Now that we know what role the factoring company plays, you can see why it might be beneficial for you to have access to your driver's account with them. There are a number of credit checks that may need to be run before you find a suitable load and then the process of uploading the documents can save the driver time.

They may also offer load advances that they driver might need to take advantage of. Again, you could request this for them if that's something you're offering.

Now we'll look at the invoicing aspect real quick.

Invoicing Life-Cycle:
- Driver has delivered load and submitted all proof with documents to the factoring company
- Factoring company has paid the driver for the load (minus their fees)

- Now the factoring company, the driver or the dispatcher must request that the broker pay the factoring company
- If the factoring company will be submitting the invoice, they already have everything they need to do so
- If the driver wishes to do this, they also have everything they need
- If you, as the Dispatcher do this, you will need to generate an invoice in the following manner below (do not use Paypal because you are not requesting money for yourself, you can use their format as a template if you'd like).
- Once the broker receives the invoice, they will pay the factoring company in whatever timeframe was established and that load payment cycle is complete

You can find an Invoice template in Microsoft Word or create one in a neat, presentable, professional manner and be sure to include all of the following in the invoice:

Make sure your invoice includes:

An Invoice# - this can be in whatever sequence you decide, make sure you use a system to where it will be easy to locate them if necessary

List the **Name of the Trucking Company and MC#** somewhere in bold

State to 'Remit Payment to' - Name and Address of the factoring company (be sure it's the address designated for payments because they may have more than one address)

List the 'Bill to' - Name and Address of Broker. Again, be sure it's the one they provided for payment requests. This is usually always in the carrier packet you filled out with the broker and on the Rate Con

Invoice Date - the date you're sending the invoice

Load Number/Reference Number from the Rate Con that identifies the load

In the **Invoice Summary Section** - List the load amount and any additional fees such as Lumper fees that we discussed earlier. Then have a field for the Total amount

Notice of Assignment Section - Here is where you'll have a few sentences that say that the Carrier has sold the invoice and assigned the factoring company as the payee and that payment must be remitted to that factoring company

You can also include any email, ACH or Wire Payment Information, Overnight Payment Information and re-type the address for **all options the broker can use to send their payment**

Add a Thank You For Your Business at the bottom in bold and that's about all you need. Email the invoice to the broker, with the Rate Con and BOL attached.

Just be mindful of keying in all information correctly. As I stated earlier, if the Broker doesn't pay the factoring company, the driver may be liable so stay on top of ensuring that the invoices are getting paid on.

At this point in our business, almost 2 years as I'm updating this book, we've had situations where we were short paid by a broker. In this instance, the broker paid the factoring company, but they didn't pay the full amount on a load for whatever reason. We had to get in touch with the broker and see if they needed additional paperwork. Sometimes they'll just email and ask for all the paperwork on the load. Maybe something wasn't legible or a clear picture or if you made a mistake and send the wrong BOL, like the unsigned one. It could be a number of reasons. But once it gets fixed, they'll pay, and you should be fine.

We've had times when our load payout was not the full amount because of one of these issues. But once it's resolved, they'll pay it on another later load later on down the line.

On the next page I'll insert a screenshot of an invoice that our factoring company generated for us and sent to the broker that we moved a load for.

BlackLight Logistics LLC

Invoice #155766

Remit to:
Freight Factoring Corp.
PO Box 2███████████
Dallas, TX 75320-6773

C/o: BlackLight Logistics LLC
MC: ███████████

Bill to:
The ████████████pany
▪▪▪ █████ Ave
Indianapolis, IN 46202

Invoice Date	Load No / Ref #
12/19/2020	155766

Load details

Trips	Date
Shipper1: U-Haul Moving & Storage of ███████████	12/21/2020
Consignee1: U-Haul Moving & Storage of KEN, Kennesaw, GA	12/22/2020

Invoice summary

Description	Amount
Load Amount	$1,100.00
Total	**$1,100.00**

Notice of Assignment

We are pleased to advise that to enable the Carrier to better service its customers, the Carrier has assigned its present and future accounts receivable to us. This invoice has been sold, assigned, and must be made payable to:

Freight Factoring Corp.
PO Box ███████████
Dallas, TX 75320-6773 Any claims or offset must be reported immediately to (800)███████████. Payment to any other party does not constitute payment.

ACH and Wire Payments
Freight Factoring Corp.
Recipient Institution: Wells Fargo
ABA Routing Number ███████████
Account Number ███████████
Swift Number: ███████████ payment)

Overnight Payment
Lockbox Services
███████████actoring Corp.
███████████
Irving, TX 75063

Thank you for your business!

A few of those Big Brokerages that will work with new authority (as of the time we got started), in case you need it:

1. TQL

2. Landstar

3. Fifth Wheel Freight

4. CH Robinson

5. Knight Logistics

6. OTR Freight – I believe they will if the driver is factoring with them.

7. DOFT

For these big ones, you usually have to sign up on an online registration platform and then the processing can take a few days. Sometimes it can be within the same day if you have a load. So if your driver is new, do this right away so that you have some other options besides pulling from the DAT load board. These brokerages all have their own load boards so you can be looking at all of them.

If you're just starting out and have any questions about anything I've gone over in this book and you want some advice or guidance, I do offer home business startup coaching and consultations 😎

You can get some details on my other site here: https://halalhomebusiness.com

Okay that's all of my random extra thoughts. Time to get to those resources:

The dispatching course I took...they allowed for monthly payments, and they were very thorough with great customer service. You can click on it...

https://learndispatch.teachable.com/?affcode=32879_fahcvncd

This is an affiliate link but if you can't click or copy/paste, no biggie, just go straight to their site at www.learndispatch.com Should be easy enough to remember.

If you thought this was thorough and you'd like to see that over-the-shoulder look of how I use the apps on a day-to-day basis, you can go to this mini-eourse. I created it for people to look over my shoulder in short videos to get your daily set-up together. Click the link

https://blacklightlogistics.thinkific.com

Visit our site for free resources for your drivers. To date we have one for helping prepare for the new entrant audit and with finding a factoring company. https://blacklightlogisticsllc.com

For more tips about trucking and dispatching, come join my new YouTube family. I make videos about home businesses and marketing. I've recently separated all of my trucking content just for ya'll! Come check it out @BlackLight Logistics

Wishing you the best on your journey with your trucking company or your dispatching business!

Thank you for supporting our Veteran-Owned, Black-Owned Business

www.ingramcontent.com/pod-product-compliance
Lightning Source LLC
Chambersburg PA
CBHW071128240526
45465CB00024B/1547